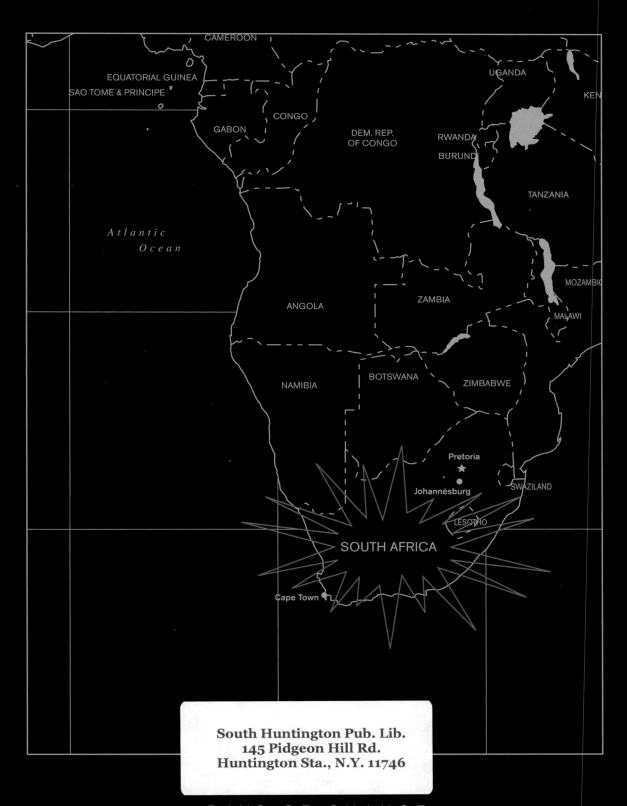

CAMEROON

EQUATORIAL GUINEA
SAO TOME & PRINCIPE

UGANDA

KEN

GABON

CONGO

DEM. REP.
OF CONGO

RWANDA
BURUNDI

TANZANIA

*Atlantic
Ocean*

MOZAMBIQ

ANGOLA

ZAMBIA

MALAWI

NAMIBIA

BOTSWANA

ZIMBABWE

Pretoria
★
●
Johannesburg

SWAZILAND

LESOTHO

SOUTH AFRICA

Cape Town

DAYS OF CHANGE

☾ *Creative Education*

BY KATE RIGGS

Published by Creative Education
P.O. Box 227, Mankato, Minnesota 56002
Creative Education is an imprint of The Creative Company
www.thecreativecompany.us

Cover design and art direction by Rita Marshall
Interior design and book production by The Design Lab
Printed in the United States of America

Photographs by AP Images (Ron Frehm, Pool, Homer Smith),
Corbis (Bettmann, Kevin Carter/Megan Patricia Carter Trust/
Sygma, Gallo Images, Wally McNamee, Gideon Mendel,
JUDA NGWENYA/Reuters, David Turnley, Peter Turnley),
Getty Images (AFP, MARGARET BOURKE-WHITE, WALTER
DHLADHLA/AFP, ALEXANDER JOE/AFP, Cynthia Johnson//
Time & Life Pictures, GERARD JULIEN/AFP, Frank Micelotta,
Popperfoto, Jurgen Schadeberg/Hulton Archive, Terrence
Spencer//Time & Life Pictures, Selwyn Tait//Time & Life
Pictures, Grey Villet//Time & Life Pictures) iStockphoto

Library of Congress Cataloging-in-Publication Data
Riggs, Kate.
The release of Nelson Mandela / by Kate Riggs.
p. cm. – (Days of change)
Includes bibliographical references and index.
ISBN 978-1-58341-736-2
1. Mandela, Nelson, (1918–)–Juvenile literature. 2. Mandela,
Nelson, (1918–)–Imprisonment–Juvenile literature. 3.
Presidents–South Africa–Biography–Juvenile literature. I.
Title. II. Series.
DT1974.R54 2009
365'.45092–dc22   2008009168
[B]

First Edition
9 8 7 6 5 4 3 2 1

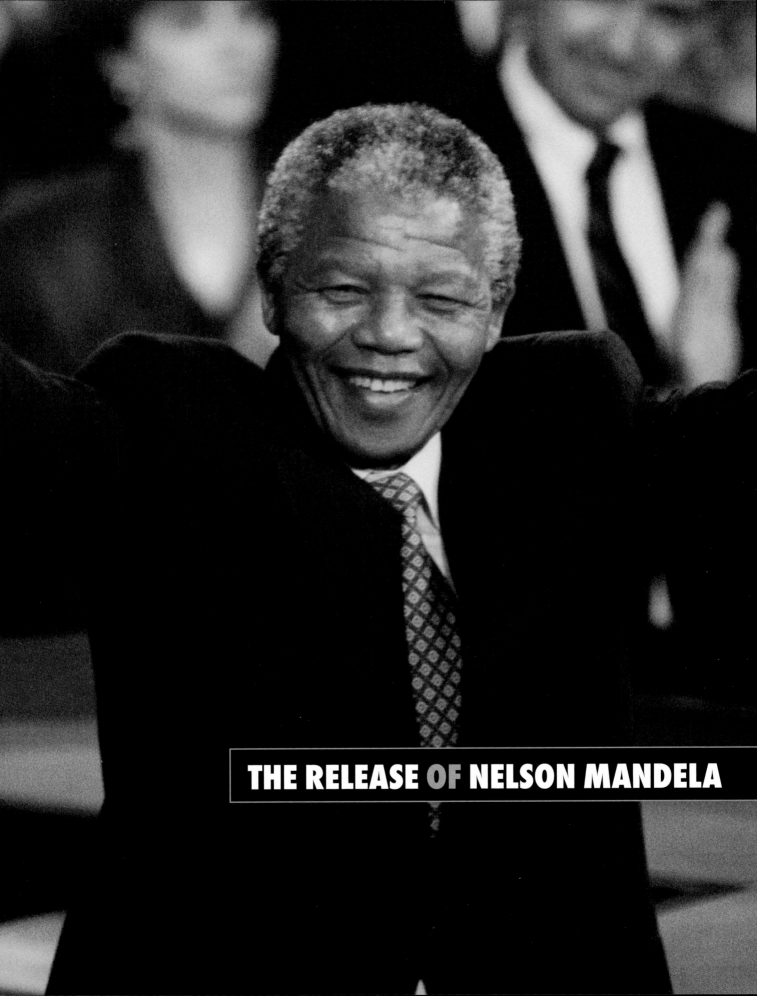

THE RELEASE OF NELSON MANDELA

Nelson Mandela and his second wife Winnie Madikizela-Mandela led a procession of proud supporters as Nelson was released from Victor Verster Prison in February 1990.

As he walked out the gates of Victor Verster Prison near Paarl, South Africa, 71-year-old Nelson Mandela gripped the hand of his wife Winnie and squinted into a sunny, cloudless sky. After 27 years, the most famous prisoner in the world was finally free. The road leading to freedom had been long and trying, but on February 11, 1990, Mandela was allowed to walk among his people for the first time since being sentenced to life in prison in 1964.

Hundreds of photographers, reporters, and well-wishers greeted a stunned Mandela at the prison gates. The enthusiastic crowd was only a taste of what was to come, and Mandela realized that he was not sufficiently prepared to grasp the full significance of what his release meant to people—in South Africa and throughout the world. As he raised a triumphant fist in the air, the crowd roared, cameras clicked, and television crews recorded the joyous scene. A new life was beginning for Nelson Mandela, but as he embarked on the journey to lead South Africa toward a more democratic and equal government, he realized that he would experience a new, more positive kind of imprisonment. This time, he would be held captive and accountable by an entire nation.

February 11, 1990

When Nelson Rolihlahla Mandela was born on July 18, 1918, parts of South Africa were still controlled by traditional tribal systems run by chiefs and their councils. Mandela was himself the son of a hereditary chief in a region called the Transkei, and he spent his childhood training to take his place in the tribal leadership. The Transkei had become part of the British colony of South Africa only eight years before Mandela's birth, and it was an attractive place for native Africans to live. In the Transkei, natives were allowed to own land, a right that was diminishing elsewhere in South Africa.

At the national level, people of Dutch and British backgrounds ruled South Africa. Dutch traders from Holland had settled in South Africa in the late 1600s, and when Britain claimed the land as a colony in the early 1800s, South Africa's economy and government became a mix of both countries' influences. Through military force, Britain soon began taking away more land from native Africans, and wars erupted throughout the colony during the 1800s.

Descendants of the Dutch settlers, who were known as Afrikaners, had a powerful voice in South Africa's government, which was controlled by both the British and Afrikaners. These white people were the minority in South Africa, yet most did not want the native Africans and people of other cultures and ethnic backgrounds to have any say in politics.

Mandela belonged to a generation of Africans who were educated at English-speaking, Christian schools and resented the white government's suppression of native people. For most

A NATION DIVIDED

6

Bordering the Indian Ocean on the southeastern coast of South Africa, the Transkei is
a farming region that benefits from the rivers that flow from the mountains to the sea.

8

blacks, it was not possible to receive a good education or adequate health care because of where they lived. Blacks were separated from whites and restricted from living or traveling in certain areas by a system of pass laws. Every nonwhite South African was required to carry a document called a pass book to prove that he or she was allowed to be moving between areas that were designated for blacks or whites only.

Man holding his pass book

In 1912, black Africans created their own political party, the African National Congress (ANC), which was in need of fresh leadership by 1940, when Mandela began his political career. He and a group of other young adults decided that they would bring the ANC into a more direct relationship with the government, a relationship in which the opinions of the ANC would be valued. To accomplish this, Mandela moved to the city of Johannesburg in 1941. At that time, the city of Johannesburg was experiencing growth in its economy. Because South Africa had joined Britain in the fight against Nazi Germany in World War II, blacks were able to find more jobs (since the whites were elsewhere fighting), and the region's wealth was growing. The rules of segregation relaxed, and more blacks moved into urban areas from rural townships. This great migration did not make the majority of Afrikaners happy.

In 1940, Johannesburg was the financial center of the country and was rapidly becoming South Africa's richest and most modern city, complete with tall office buildings and bustle.

"A doctrine of hate can never take people anywhere. It is too exacting. It warps the mind. That is why we preach the doctrine of love, love for Africa. We can never do enough for Africa, nor can we love her enough. The more we do for her, the more we wish to do. And I am sure I am speaking for the whole of young Africa when I say that we are prepared to work with any man who is fighting for the liberation of Africa within our lifetime."

ROBERT SOBUKWE,
first president of the
Pan Africanist Congress
(PAC), 1949

During the 1950s, Mandela and friend Oliver Tambo ran the firm Mandela and Tambo,
the first all-black law practice in South Africa to offer free or low-cost legal counsel.

After World War II ended, the South African government instituted a system called apartheid, making even more laws that were based on race. Blacks were restricted to living in separate parts of cities, groomed for certain jobs and barred from others, and prevented from obtaining full citizenship by an increasingly complex set of laws. Mandela and such friends as Oliver Tambo and Walter Sisulu knew that such unfairness on the basis of race was wrong. Tambo and Mandela, who were trained as lawyers, later based their law practice on helping blacks overcome discrimination.

Mandela worked to gather support for the ANC among other blacks, people with Indian and Asian backgrounds, and white communists. The Communist Party of South Africa was founded in 1921, but it did not gain much political power until it aligned itself with the ANC in the 1940s. Mandela felt that the communists were important allies to have. The inclusion of communists not only influenced the ANC to become more multiracial, but it also brought a more socialist approach to the way the ANC led its campaigns for governmental reform. The theory of socialism called for communities to share power and possessions so that no individual could have complete control over the production of goods, the making of laws, or any other part of the society.

"There never was any kind of life I can recall as family life, a young bride's life where you sit with your husband. You just couldn't tear Nelson from the people: the struggle, the nation came first."

WINNIE MADIKIZELA-MANDELA, Mandela's second wife

11

It was a dangerous time to be a communist, though. After World War II ended, the United States and the Soviet Union became the main players in a conflict that would span almost 50 years—the Cold War. Because communists ran the Soviet Union, and the U.S. was a democracy, the Cold War also became a war between two styles of government, and communism was seen as a major threat by the U.S. and western Europe. Any country reforming its government at that time was encouraged by the West to implement a democratic, rather than a communistic, one. Those countries that were communist—such as Cuba and China—banded together against the democracies, and a worldwide battle over ideas and policies was waged.

By 1950, the Cold War was in full swing, and Mandela's political career experienced a turning point. He was thrust into the spotlight of the ANC as an elected official of the National Executive,

On June 26, 1955, an event called the Congress of the People was held in Kliptown. Mandela was banned from attending, but he was there, dressed in a disguise. He watched as 3,000 delegates from all over South Africa were introduced to a document called the Freedom Charter. The Charter proclaimed that all South Africans had a right to a free and representative government. In April 1956, the ANC approved the Charter, sending a clear message to the Afrikaner government that there was a strong anti-racial movement afoot in the country. June 26 is now celebrated in South Africa annually as Freedom Day.

The ANC brought together South Africans of all ethnicities to protest in large numbers against the government policies of apartheid that gripped their country in the mid-1950s.

At the same time that Mandela and members of the ANC were trying to revolutionize South Africa, other countries around the world were also experiencing upheaval. The South Africans were inspired by the success stories of Mao Zedong in China and Fidel Castro in Cuba—Castro in particular became a revolutionary role model for Mandela. From 1957 to 1959, Castro had also led a fairly small group in a militant strike against his government until he succeeded in overthrowing an unpopular leader. Although Castro later instituted a strict communist dictatorship and fell out of favor with Western countries, Mandela always considered him a friend.

Mandela was unflappable during the lengthy Treason Trial, which lasted from 1956 to 1961 and acquitted all accused, and he soon became even more involved in anti-apartheid efforts.

the ruling body. He became more active in protesting the policies of the Afrikaner government and working to change the course of apartheid. However, such increased visibility soon made Mandela a target of the Afrikaners, and during the late 1950s and early 1960s, he had to keep his work against the government as secretive as possible. He was even banned from giving public speeches after the Afrikaners figured out how effectively he could nonviolently mobilize people against them.

On December 5, 1956, Mandela was arrested on charges of treason. The lengthy "Treason Trial" that followed brought all 156 of the accused (which included almost the entire leadership of the ANC and South Africa's other non-Afrikaner political parties) closer together, no matter the differences in their races and backgrounds. It showed them as no other event could have how important it was for nonwhite South Africans to remain a united front against a government bent on segregating them.

Although he was cleared by the Treason Trial, Mandela had no intentions of ending his involvement with the ANC. Instead, he decided that he would be able to work most effectively for change by disappearing underground, or going into hiding. As

"He was probably the most wanted man in the country at the time, and was taking great risks. But that was his style. He was one who led from the front. He never asked anyone to take a risk which he was not prepared to take first for himself."

RUSTY BERNSTEIN, former communist member of the ANC, 1999

15

his friend and fellow ANC leader Walter Sisulu later explained, Mandela's decision to go underground was a dangerous one that everyone involved knew could end only in jail time. "When we decided that he should go underground, I knew that he was now stepping into a position of leadership. . . . We had got the leadership outside [with Oliver Tambo in London, England] but we must have a leader in jail."

While he was in hiding for 17 months, beginning in early 1961, Mandela listened to the cries of his people for action. They were increasingly frustrated by the fact that nonviolent forms of protest against the government seemed to have no effect, and they demanded a change to violence instead. Mandela formed a military wing of the ANC called Umkhonto we Sizwe (abbreviated to MK and translated to mean "Spear of the Nation") and became its commander. Newspapers began calling him the "Black Pimpernel" while he was

Racial segregation had been a part of South Africa's government and culture long before the Afrikaner National Party instituted apartheid in 1948. The pass laws begun by colonial governments in the late 1700s and upheld through the 1940s formed part of the basis for segregationist policies. But the National Party further separated the races when it passed the Population Registration Act of 1950. This law required every South African to tell the government what his or her race was and made it possible for the Afrikaners to enact even stronger policies against blacks, Coloureds (people of mixed races), and Asians (those of Indian and Pakistani descent).

As a form of protest, native South Africans gathered to burn their pass books in 1960—a year fraught with tension between the white and nonwhite populations of the country.

The dead and wounded—many of whom were shot in the back as they turned to run—lay on the ground outside the Sharpeville police station following the 1960 massacre.

The Sharpeville massacre of March 21, 1960, began as a protest against carrying pass books, or documents that said that a nonwhite South African was allowed to move about the country. To peacefully protest this example of apartheid, about 10,000 to 20,000 people surrounded the police station in Sharpeville. The police became nervous, looking out at such a large crowd of people who they perceived to be a threat. They started firing into the crowd of unarmed citizens, and 69 people were killed. The incident turned the world's attention on apartheid, but it would be 26 years before the discriminatory pass laws were finally repealed.

in hiding, publicizing his disappearance and drawing attention to him.

Mandela dodged the South African police for months, traveling as far away as London to meet with prominent people sympathetic to the South African cause. He spent much of his time networking and gaining support for the ANC. He also sought donations of guns and other weapons for MK's use and helped set up a training site for MK activists. Everyone encouraged him to stay abroad instead of risk capture at home. But Mandela returned to South Africa in 1962, and this time, he would not escape.

On Sunday, August 5, 1962, Nelson Mandela was arrested while on his way from his hideout near Rivonia to Johannesburg. He was charged with incitement to strike and leaving the country without a passport. Mandela defended himself at his trial and called no witnesses, leaving time for an hour-long speech in which he explained how his political beliefs had compelled him to help nonwhite South Africans gain a voice in their government. He believed that he had become a living symbol of the people's struggle for freedom and democracy and of what they could accomplish. He was sentenced to five years imprisonment, the first year of which he spent at a prison in nearby Pretoria and on Robben Island, an infamous dumping ground for all of South Africa's political prisoners.

THE PRICE OF FREEDOM

In the meantime, the South African government cracked down on the ANC leadership in hiding, eventually uncovering their Rivonia safe haven. The government seized documents that incriminated Mandela further as the leader of MK and instigator of violent acts (such as bombings) against the government, and the new charges of sabotage turned his five-year sentence into a much bleaker picture. The new trial opened in November 1963. The evidence against him, largely in the form of his handwritten letters and documented plans, was insurmountable, and Mandela accepted the consequences. The sentence was life in prison.

Mandela returned to Robben Island in June 1964, where prisoners routinely experienced severe beatings and strict segregation by race. A few

20

G.P.-S.6128—1956-7—130,000. S.

U.D.J. 315.

Senior Publieke aanklaer

Aan

Die Magistraat, distrik *Johannesburg*

Die Vrederegter, wyk_____, distrik_____

Aansoek ingevolge artikel 28 van Wet No. 56 van 1955 om Bevelskrif tot Inhegtenis neming.

Hierby word aansoek gedoen om uitreiking van 'n bevelskrif ot inhegtenis-

neming van NELSON MANDELA op 'n beskuldiging van

CA 2 121·8/1953

aangesien daar volgens beëdigde verklaring redelike gronde vir verdenking teen ~~haes~~ hom

bestaan dat die beweerde ~~oortreding~~ misdaad begaan is op of omtrent die Periode 26·3·61—

9·5·61. in die distrik JOHANNESBURG

(wyk_____), of dat dit bekend is of vermoed word dat

genoemde BESK. op die oomblik in die distrik JOHANNE sb

(wyk_____) is.

_____ Staatsaanklaer.

The warrant for Mandela's arrest, issued in May 1961, more than a year before he was taken into custody, is now on display at the farm in Rivonia that served as his hideout.

days after arriving at Robben Island, Mandela and other ANC leaders (who had also been convicted by the documents found at their secret headquarters) such as Walter Sisulu were moved to a new, stark facility that was separate from the structure that housed the common criminals. For the next 18 years, Mandela would call an 8-by-7-foot (2.4 by 2.1 m) cell home.

At first, the prisoners were not allowed to talk to each other. They kept quiet while they pounded rocks into gravel in the prison courtyard for hours on end and while they worked in the lime quarry, hacking away rock to dig out the lime. They were silenced even when they washed or ate meals.

ANC activist Walter Sisulu

They were isolated in every sense and were not permitted contact with the outside world either.

As the years passed, restrictions were relaxed and conversations started. Since all of the political prisoners (about 30) were isolated from the rest of the prison populace, they had a unique opportunity to get to know and respect one another, even though some were from different political parties such as the communists. Mandela had the company of some of his closest friends, but he also wanted to open the lines of communication between the different races and political groups, optimistically hoping it would foster greater cooperation on the outside.

Tourists to the prison-turned-museum can see what Mandela's barren cell at Robben Island looked like before he was issued a bed in 1978 and a table and bookshelves in later years.

"What amazed me about Nelson and [Walter] Sisulu and other people who had life sentences was the calmness, the equanimity with which they led their prison lives. They didn't throw in the towel. They didn't display bitterness. They showed me how to laugh at the tortures we went through."

SONNY VENKATRATHNAM, fellow prisoner with Mandela, 1995

In Northern Ireland, fighting between political factions raged from 1968 to 1998. The Provisional Irish Republican Army (PIRA) wanted Northern Ireland to gain independence from Great Britain and be united with Ireland. Loyalists, however, wanted to remain under British rule. Mandela himself encouraged the groups to simply sit down and agree to talk to each other, as that would be the only way to find a path to peace. He was right. In 1998, the PIRA and Loyalists signed an agreement that allowed both sides to compromise peacefully, and they went on to form a cooperative government that greatly resembled South Africa's under Mandela.

Mandela encouraged an educational atmosphere at the prison, and the prisoners ran a university of sorts, with anyone who had a degree teaching his subject to the others. In prison, there was much time for self-reflection and study, and Mandela learned new skills that went beyond academics. By controlling his temper, developing greater persuasive language skills, and listening to everyone, he exerted his influence over his fellow prisoners and their Afrikaner guards, called warders. It was in prison that Mandela learned how to be an effective politician.

By 1975, the prisoners' diets had improved, the assaults by warders had grown infrequent, and the inmates had even been given a tennis court in the yard. But nothing could take the prisoners' minds off of the lives they had left behind. Mandela felt increasingly estranged from his family; his four children had grown up without him, and he missed his wife Winnie terribly.

Meanwhile, it was as if the Western world had forgotten all about the struggle that had put Mandela and the others on Robben Island. Britain essentially turned a blind eye to South Africa's apartheid and militaristic government, not wanting to harm its economic relationship with the country, as South Africa

"[Nelson Mandela's] achievement has been dependent on mastering politics in its broadest and longest sense, on understanding how to move and persuade people, to change their attitudes. He has always been determined, like [Mahatma] Gandhi or [Winston] Churchill, to lead from the front, through his example and presence; and he learned early how to build up and understand his own image."

ANTHONY SAMPSON, British journalist and historian, 1999

25

was a valued trading partner in mining products such as gold. America was preoccupied with its Cold War-fueled conflict in Vietnam, and U.S. politicians did little more than talk about the evils of apartheid—taking no action to stop it. The ANC's ties to communist governments, such as those of the Soviet Union and China, were thereby strengthened, and the communists became virtually the only ones who offered help to the ANC.

After 18 years on Robben Island, Mandela, Sisulu, and two other prisoners were abruptly moved to Pollsmoor Prison near the Cape Town suburb of Tokai in 1982. Conditions there were much improved, with more nutritious meals and access to newspapers, radio, and even television, which they had never seen before. Although they were hardly allowed outside, Mandela was permitted to start a rooftop garden, in which he

A visual reminder of the Cold War's divisiveness, the Berlin Wall was built to separate the eastern and western parts of the city of Berlin, Germany, in 1961. Following World War II, East Germany was controlled by the communist Soviet Union, while West Germany was influenced and supported by Western governments in Europe and America. Before the wall was built, about 2.5 million people escaped East Germany and found refuge in the more attractive and economically successful West Germany. In 1989, shortly before Mandela was released, the Berlin Wall was torn down, and the "iron curtain" of the Cold War was officially lifted.

Native South Africans were often moved by the government from their home regions to locations near diamond mines to provide a workforce for the country's most profitable industry.

In 1985, groups of demonstrators went so far as to brave police reactions in an effort to get Mandela and other political prisoners released from Pollsmoor Prison in Cape Town.

eventually had 900 plants. But the four men, separated from their comrades and from the political progress they had been making amongst the inmates on the island, were agitated in their isolation.

A serious effort to get Mandela released from prison had begun in 1980. The ANC was increasingly desperate to promote a leader who had the standing to reform the apartheid-riddled government, and Mandela's influence was still felt among the community through letters he wrote to those on the outside. By 1985, South African president P. W. Botha listened to the plea to release Mandela. He offered Mandela his freedom if Mandela promised to call off MK's violent retaliations (which usually took the form of bombings and targeted killings) against government buildings and officials. Botha was certain that his plan was brilliant, but his confidence was premature; Mandela rejected the bargain and issued a statement declaring that

29

Botha was the one who should promise to stop the cycle of violence by ending apartheid, thus ending the people's protests against it.

Mandela had become the most famous prisoner in the world, and Botha knew that he must handle the situation carefully. Riots were already breaking out in large cities such as Johannesburg, and people frustrated by the stubbornness of the Afrikaner government were turning to more and more violent means of expression, such as using car bombs in public places. The violence hurt South Africa's economy as well, since the country counted on investments from Western countries such as the U.S. and Britain to keep it afloat. Once Westerners lost confidence in the government's ability to control its people, they stopped funding businesses. The government, which had been overspending on the military and in other areas as well, was fighting to uphold apartheid and going into serious debt at the same time.

From the car bombings in Pretoria in 1983 to other isolated instances throughout the 1980s,
South Africa was rocked by numerous acts of violence carried out in the ANC's name.

Like Mandela, Frederik Willem (F. W.) de Klerk began his career in politics with a background in law. A successful practicing attorney in the industrial city of Vereeniging, south of Johannesburg, de Klerk became involved with the Afrikaner National Party in the 1970s. He had such high standing within the party, in fact, that he was elected party leader in 1989 when President P. W. Botha fell ill and could no longer perform his duties. De Klerk was then appointed president by the parliament, the governing body which, at the time, represented only a fraction of South Africa's population.

When he was sworn in as South Africa's president in September 1989, F. W. de Klerk was poised to end apartheid, calling for a united government and a new constitution.

As Mandela continued working with the government to negotiate his release, he was moved to increasingly better facilities. Shortly after Mandela was moved to a comfortable warder's house at the Victor Verster Prison near Paarl, Botha suffered a stroke in January 1989. His replacement was a politician named F. W. de Klerk, and it was de Klerk who now had to decide what to do about Mandela. Mandela had been talking privately with government officials for several months, trying to make a deal for his release. Part of his plan was accomplished when Sisulu and seven other prominent political prisoners were unexpectedly released in late 1989. Mandela was now the only one who remained.

De Klerk addressed the parliament, the governing body of South Africa, on the opening day of its new session, February 2, 1990. To the shock of fellow Afrikaners, he revealed that life as they knew it would be changing dramatically and that he had agreed to release Nelson Mandela in nine days' time. The atmosphere in South Africa changed almost overnight. Nonwhite South Africans began to hope that the days of apartheid were finally numbered. On February 11, 1990, the world watched as Mandela was released at the gates of Victor Verster Prison.

"There was a tremendous surge of feeling. Like many others I'd lost friends and neighbors to political violence during the dark years of apartheid. The hope for the future that I and so many others felt that day rippled through the crowd. The branches of the trees in front of the Town Hall were stripped by people climbing them to get a better view. People were literally falling from the trees, which began to resemble bare scarecrows."

RICHARD RAMSDEN, witness of Mandela's release, 1990

33

Once he was released from prison, Nelson Mandela was free to become the leader his people had thought was lost. But he first had to convince de Klerk and the Afrikaners that the ANC deserved to be a recognized part of the government. (The ANC had been banned by the Afrikaners in 1960 and had been operating underground since then.) Mandela traveled the world in the six months following his release. He raised awareness and funds

BUILDING A LEGACY

for the party and caught up on the life that he had missed in the past 27 years. He also became deputy president of the ANC, not wanting to take over completely while he was still adjusting to life outside prison walls. The following year, he replaced his old friend Oliver Tambo as ANC president and moved forward in his joint work with de Klerk to achieve a peaceful end to apartheid.

Everywhere he went, Mandela commanded respect from world leaders such as U.S. president George H. W. Bush, French president François Mitterrand, and England's Queen Elizabeth II. Oddly enough, as historian Anthony Sampson has noted, "while he was acclaimed throughout the world as the great liberator, the new Moses or Messiah, he had no tangible power inside his own country, and no convincing liberation army." Mandela's strong belief that South Africa would soon become a democracy was convincing enough for most people, though. Once apartheid was dismantled, he expected that the next logical step for South Africa to take would be to embrace a demo-

34

Mandela's travels continued after he was elected president, and he met with leaders such as U.S. president Bill Clinton and Speaker of the House Newt Gingrich in the late 1990s.

As part of his post-prison tour around the world, Mandela addressed the United Nations'
Special Committee against Apartheid at its New York City headquarters in June 1990.

cratic system of government. And he knew that the country would need help from the international community to make that happen.

Mandela was in favor of nationalizing businesses, or having them controlled and owned collectively by the government. But private business owners were not enthused about such a prospect, so Mandela became more flexible. He offered a compromise that would help protect South African investments and would also allow for businesses to continue operating in a more capitalist society. Under capitalism, businesses could be owned by private individuals or companies and make their own profits, instead of being forced to work for a national government that would distribute the profits among the people.

Many nonwhite South Africans felt a strong, negative connection between capitalism and oppression, since capitalism was the system they had known previously under apartheid, and Mandela himself was more attracted to the profit-sharing of socialism. But the world had changed, and nations' economies had become more globalized and interdependent because they were all based primarily on capitalism. The only successful way to conduct national (and

"The ANC is a great deal more than a political party. Representing as it does the great majority of articulate Africans in the Union, it is almost the parliament of a nation. A nation without a state, perhaps, but it is as a nation that the Africans increasingly think of themselves."

T. W. L. MacDermot, Canadian High Commissioner in Cape Town, 1953

37

international) business in the 1990s was through private and free enterprise—the hallmark of capitalism. So even before he took any official leadership position, Mandela worked to ensure that the new South Africa would be able to function and prosper in the new business climate.

During the period of time between Mandela's release and South Africa's first free elections in 1994, violence continued to escalate throughout the country, as the tensions that had been brewing for the past 30 years boiled over. Not all South Africans wanted to be united and work together under a leader such as Mandela. Many native African tribes had been content to remain separate from white South Africans, and they had benefited from the apartheid system in some measure. Yet political violence among the native Zulu people was particularly difficult to ignore, as a total of 3,653 people died between 1990 and 1993. Such violence among native Africans at times seemed to be backed in part by some factions of the white government, which often supplied arms to some tribes to provoke others, thwarting the ANC's claim that it could govern peacefully over all groups in South Africa.

"He symbolizes a much broader forgiveness and understanding and reaching out. If he had come out of prison and sent a different message, I can tell you this country could be in flames. . . . He knew exactly the way he wanted to come out, but also the way he addressed the people from the beginning, sending the message of what he thought was the best way to save lives in this country, to bring reconciliation. . . . Some people criticize that he went too far. There is no such thing as going too far if you are trying to save this country from this kind of tragedy."

GRAÇA MACHEL, Mandela's third wife, 1998

The Truth and Reconciliation Commission (TRC) was established by the ANC and Mandela in 1995 and began its work in February 1996. Its purpose was to get to the bottom of who was at fault for the atrocities (such as organized killings and strategic bombings) committed in the name of apartheid or political progress in the past 30 years. Its success depended on people volunteering to come forward and confess their involvement; a confession then protected them against further legal action. The information gathering and findings of the TRC were controversial but also effective, revealing truths about the darker dealings of such groups as the ANC and the Afrikaners.

Members of the Zulu tribe resisted the ANC's efforts to include them in the new South African government, preferring instead to be led by the often-militant Inkatha Freedom Party.

In the weeks leading up to the historic elections of April 27, 1994, thousands of people showed their support for Mandela's candidacy at mass rallies held by the ANC.

Still, in the midst of the mounting violence, Mandela continued his talks and negotiations with the Afrikaners, hoping to broker a deal that would result in the creation of a democracy and the end of apartheid. Mandela was always the central cog in the negotiating machine—if things ever got off track, all sides needed him in order to get back on. September 26, 1992, marked a historic summit at which Mandela and de Klerk agreed to commit to forming a unified, multiracial government based on a new constitution, or set of rules. Both wanted to make the transition to that new government as peaceful as possible.

South Africa's first fully democratic elections—open to people of all races— were scheduled for April 27, 1994. While touring the U.S. in July 1993, Mandela proudly announced, "the countdown to the democratic transfer of power to the people has begun." Still, violence continued to plague and divide South Africa.

As bombs exploded around Johannesburg in the final days before the elections, nonwhite Africans became even more determined to cast their votes for change.

The eyes of the world were now on South Africa. And no one seemed disappointed when the ANC emerged victorious in the elections and Mandela became the nation's president. Almost 63 percent of South Africans voted for the ANC, giving the party a clear majority in the new parliament. Since they had pledged to institute a unified government, Mandela and the ANC welcomed de Klerk and his National Party, along with other political parties, into the assembly of representatives who would cooperate to govern the nation. No one party dominated the others, and those who had been concerned that the communist element would take over were proven wrong.

"The history of liberation heroes shows that when they come into office they interact with powerful groups: they can easily forget that they've been put in power by the poorest of the poor. They often lose their common touch, and turn against their own people."

NELSON MANDELA, President of South Africa, 1996

Committed to improving South Africans' quality of life, Mandela worked to reform many programs such as housing, health care, and education. When a new constitution that protected all South Africans' rights first came before parliament in May 1996, Mandela helped get it approved. Unlike other African countries, such as Zimbabwe and Nigeria, that had

African countries in turmoil in the late 1900s painted foreboding pictures of what life in South Africa could have been like had it not been for Mandela's leadership. Countries that had been ruled by colonial governments were engulfed in terrible wars; in Algeria, half a million people died over the course of the Algerian War of Independence (1954–1962). The Algerians had a historically rocky relationship with France, which had occupied the northern African country since the 1800s. At first, the rebellious ANC was in for a similarly tough fight against the Afrikaners, but its later policy of reconciliation helped the ANC prevail with relatively little bloodshed.

Mandela was jubilant in his presidential victory, but he began working right away with his

In addition to sharing in the honors of the 1993 Nobel Peace Prize, de Klerk also served as one of Mandela's deputy presidents (along with Thabo Mbeki) until 1996.

For their extraordinary efforts at reaching compromises and building a more peaceful South Africa, Mandela and de Klerk were jointly awarded the Nobel Peace Prize in December 1993. The Nobel Prizes, founded by Swede Alfred Nobel and given out every year since 1901, honor people around the world who have contributed exceptional achievements to the fields of literature, physics, chemistry, and physiology or medicine, and those who have worked for peace. However, even though Mandela and de Klerk may have been outwardly peaceful toward each other, they did not enjoy a friendly relationship, and each blamed the other for certain mistakes.

recently undergone similarly vast political changes, South Africa was not showing signs of upheaval or corruption. It did not bow to any group's special interests.

South Africa's peaceful transition from a segregated state to a unified democracy convinced the international community that releasing Mandela had been the best thing that could have happened to the country. Progressive strides toward restoring peace among all citizens of South Africa were made, and many people's quality of life improved while Mandela served as president. When he had finished his five-year term in June 1999, he felt he could retire from politics in peace. He knew he had made a significant difference in the lives of his people. The 81-year-old left a legacy of forgiveness and reconciliation that he encouraged his colleagues to continue. By extending a hand of peace to former enemies, including the warders and others who had had a direct involvement in his imprisonment, Mandela taught the world that forgiveness was the path to true and lasting reconciliation. His constant acts of bravery in displaying such an open and accepting attitude served to inspire others to do the same.

The man who had remade himself into one of the foremost politicians of the 20th century while in jail for almost 30 years had also remade his homeland. By the beginning of the 21st century, South Africans were no longer experiencing the racial intolerance and violence that had been fueled by apartheid. They had responded to the conditions of racial segregation that had made their society unbearable and had actively fought to change them. All of the individuals who were involved in the struggle to reform their government contributed to the collective effort. But one man stood out from the crowd. One man had always stood out. As he looked back on that day in 1990 when he had greeted the throngs of supporters and tasted full freedom for the first time, Nelson Mandela realized that, nine years later, his ultimate dream for a free South Africa had come true.

"He did not have to show off to prove that he was a leader; it was perfectly clear to anyone that he was. He was honest about everything which had to be done, and wanted it to be done in a simple way."

BRUNO MTOLO, who was later to betray Mandela as a state witness, 1966

46

Like the white dove he released at a rally commemorating the 34th anniversary of the 1960 Sharpeville massacre, Mandela himself was also a symbol of peace to many people.

BIBLIOGRAPHY

African Dawn Touring. "Cape Town Heritage: New South Africa." CapeConnected. http://www.capetown.at/heritage/history/newSA_mandela.htm.

BBC News. "On This Day: 11 February." British Broadcasting Corporation. http://news.bbc.co.uk/onthisday/hi/dates/stories/february/11/newsid_2539000/2539947.stm.

Juckes, Tim. *Opposition in South Africa: The Leadership of Z. K. Matthews, Nelson Mandela, and Stephen Biko.* Westport, Conn.: Praeger Publishers, 1995.

Lodge, Tom. *Mandela: A Critical Life.* Oxford: Oxford University Press, 2006.

Mandela, Nelson. *Long Walk to Freedom: The Autobiography of Nelson Mandela.* Boston: Little, Brown & Company, 1994.

Sampson, Anthony. *Mandela: The Authorized Biography.* New York: Alfred A. Knopf, 1999.

INDEX